Constant Compost

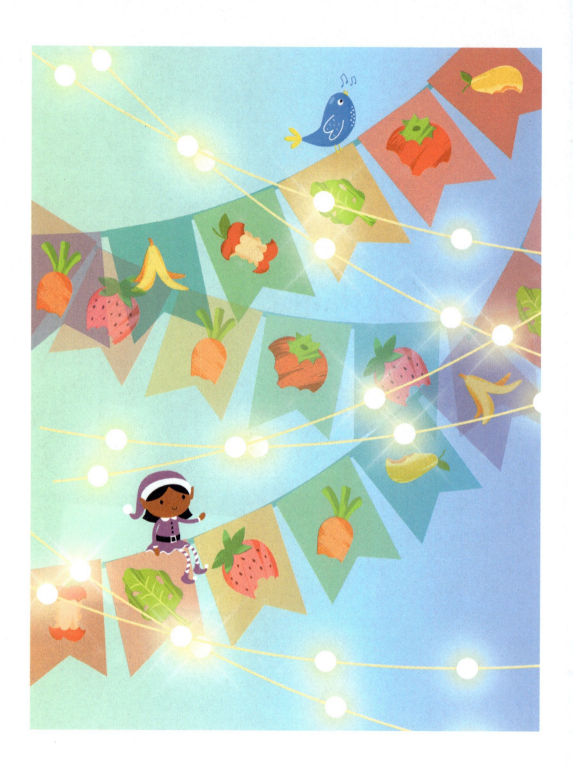

Constant Compost

How to Naturally Compost Your Food Waste Without Ever Touching a Worm

L. Moogie Christensen

Art and Cover design by L. Moogie Christensen

Copyright © 2023 L. Moogie Christensen

All rights reserved. This book or any portion may not be reproduced or used in any manner without the express written permission from the author, except for the use of brief quotations by a reviewer.

The information in this book is true and complete to the best of our knowledge. All recommendations are made without guarantee on the part of the author. The author disclaims any liability in connection with the use of this information.

L. Moogie Christensen
PO Box 4114
Citrus Heights CA 95610

MoogieChristensen@google.com

Dedicated to my friend Janet who challenged me to do better.

And to my dear wife and family for whom I want to be better everyday.

Thank you to Cindy Fazzi, Jerome Munroe, and Cathralynn Cook
for your invaluable editing and proofreading assistance.

Contents

1 - Keep it simple, easier and more fun 11
This little book is fast and easy 13
How I got to Constant Composting 22
Why food scrap composting is critical 35

2 - What is Constant Composting 39
How to use this book 41
You can't fool nature 43
How and why Constant Composting works 45
Helpful terms and concepts 47

3 - Let's make a Food Scrap Composter -
A protected gathering space for worms 49
Safety first 51
A detailed overview 51
Diagrammed instructions 57

4 - Start Composting -
Feed your soil and it will feed your plants 75
Collecting food scraps 77
What to put in your Constant Composter 79
Questions and Answers 81

5 - Happy Composting -
It doesn't have to be perfect to work 89
Happy Constant Composting 90

Bonus Compost/Garden Journal 91

It's me, your author, standing by one of my early experimental gardens. That flash of red is a prototype of my patented Origami Ruby food scrap composter. Ruby is a fully self-contained continuously fertilizing composter. It sits on top of the soil and provides the perfect environment for worms to eat up all of your food scraps and turn them into valuable fertilizer. Worms love it! The Ruby Composter is so easy; it's perfect for gardeners and non-gardeners alike.

But designing a product and getting it to market are two completely different projects. Pitchman Anthony Sullivan said that the Ruby was ahead of it's time. I hope not. Even though you can't get a Ruby right now, I want to show you how to compost your food scraps in the same easy Constantly Composting way. I will show you how you can build your own continuous food scrap composter out of used nursery pots and a few other things you might already have around the house.

con·stant
/ˈkänst(ə)nt/
adjective
adjective: constant

- occurring continuously over a period of time.

- remaining the same over a period of time.

- (of a person) unchangingly faithful and dependable.

com·post
/ˈkämˌpōst/
noun

- decayed organic material used as a plant fertilizer or soil amendment

1
Keep it Simple, Easier and More Fun

THIS LITTLE BOOK
IS FAST AND EASY LIKE COMPOSTING SHOULD BE

I have a lot to say about composting, but don't worry, I'm not going to say most of it here. This sweet simple how-to book is only about composting your food scraps with my easier, less gross method that I call Constant Composting.

Many gardeners go to a lot of trouble and expense to grow big, beautiful, healthy plants, but they don't always compost. That's really unfortunate because rich nutritious homemade worm compost is absolutely the best fertilizer that you can use. If you're throwing away your food scraps, you are throwing away the chance to turn your leftovers into what gardeners call black gold. If you have tried composting food scraps and found out the hard way that it can be time-consuming, hard work and gross, I'm here to tell you that it doesn't have to be. Composting your food waste can be very easy and so satisfying. You should try it. Let me show you how with Constant Composting.

> Don't throw away your old pots. Turn them into fertilizer factories run by free range worms.

I LOVE TO GARDEN, BUT I LOVE TO COMPOST EVEN MORE

It's miraculous how a whole plant grows from a tiny seed. But turning my potato peelings, wilted apples and rotten leftovers into beautiful black soil which then turns into brand new fruits, vegetables and flowers is next level magic! Composting also feeds all of the earthworms and other soil critters. Composting feeds the earth, and changes garbage into life.

It seems like such a small thing - recycling a few forgotten leftovers - a moldy onion, or a limp carrot, but it's small things that can make a big difference to your garden and to the planet. It also feels great!

Throwing your food scraps down the sink or into the garbage not only pollutes the water system or adds to landfill, but you are throwing money down the drain. Your food waste can become your best fertilizer, better than anything you can buy. Compost increases soil quality and fertility and helps you grow healthier, more productive plants.

Leaves make great compost but they only happen once a year. Food scraps happen every day.

Cold composting leaves is very easy to do. It's called leaf mold and it's super good for building your healthy soil.

Stuff black plastic bags full of wet leaves and close up the bags. Let them sit around until spring or until black and crumbly. Use it to make potting mix, mulch around your plants or work into the soil.

MORE SPECIFICALLY, HOMEMADE COMPOST

helps plants to be more drought tolerant. It improves soil texture, allowing the soil to hold more water and at the same time drain better. Compost helps plants develop bigger and more robust root structures that make them better able to cope with drier conditions. Compost adds fungal and microbial life to your soil that helps plants take up nutrients more efficiently even in challenging conditions, and you never know what conditions nature is going to throw at you and your garden these days.

> Trying to mix food scrap composting with yard waste composting is likely to attract unwanted guests to your compost pile.

SLOW COMPOSTING IS GOOD FOR OUR PLANET

Making compost reduces greenhouse emissions and using it helps plants grow larger, thereby taking more carbon out of the air. Stop sending your food waste to the landfill or down the garbage disposal. Even if your city has a food scrap recycling program, it takes gas to collect those scraps and your time and gas to go buy fertilizer when you could be easily making it. Plus leaving food scraps out in a bin for weekly collection really is gross. It attracts vermin such as rats and racoons, and breeds pests like flies and roaches. If you think that composting might be gross, then you are really going to hate cleaning out that nasty recycling container when you can't stand the smell any longer.

> Constant Composting fits into any gardening style whether it's highly organized or simply scattering seeds in the spring.

I'M GOING TO SHOW YOU HOW TO MAKE A FOOD SCRAP COMPOSTER

out of stuff that you may already have at home. This basic tool lets nature do all the work for you right out in your garden bed. You just throw all of your food scraps in it where they constantly compost and fertilize your plants at the same time. It's very simple. Nobody wants to have to touch a worm or any bugs. With my hands-off method, wild worms will break down your food scraps right out in the garden, so you don't have to:

- keep the worms inside your house or garage
- provide bedding for them
- sift through the worm poo (fertilizer) to get the good stuff out
- hire a sitter for them when you go on vacation
- worry that they will escape when they accidentally get too hot, too wet or too dry.

BY BEING ABLE TO GO IN AND OUT OF THE BIN WHENEVER THEY WANT, the worms can regulate their own comfort. They also distribute their fertilizer right into your garden bed where your plants can use it whenever they need it. You also get extra worm castings fertilizer deposited in the special collection bin that can be easily dumped out a few times a year and used wherever you want some extra fertilizer. We are going to let the worms do all of the hard and icky work for you. I'm going to show you how easy and not-gross it is to feed your soil so that it can feed your plants.

HOW I GOT TO CONSTANT COMPOSTING FOOD SCRAPS

I don't find composting unbearably gross. I only know that composting is too gross for most people because my friend Janet told me so. I knew that it could be kind of icky sometimes but I thought that because there are so many benefits, people would just do it anyway.

ONE FINE SUMMER DAY, AS I WAS YAMMERING ON AND ON

to my friend Janet about how amazingly wonderful composting is and how it's the answer to all of life's problems and the solution to peace on earth, and so on, my friend Janet said in her "please-for-the-love-of-God-stop-talking-about-this" voice, that she would compost "IF IT WEREN'T SO GROSS!" That not only shut me up, wondering if it was true, but it got me thinking: could I make composting less gross for people like my friend Janet? Could I also make it less work and less time-consuming? Because let's face it, even though I love composting, I don't have the time or the desire to babysit my garbage. When I'm not working, getting ready for work or resting from having worked all week, I also love cooking, kayaking, crafting, board games and spending some time with my family which includes any number of cats at any given time. And I'm sure that you are just as busy as I am, if not more so.

> It doesn't make sense to compost in one spot and then haul the finished compost to the plants. That wastes much of the nutrition where nothing is growing. Compost next to your plants.

WHILE TRYING
TO FIGURE OUT HOW

to make composting less gross and easier over the years, I have done a lot of research and experimenting. Many of my trials turned into errors in actual practice. But that's OK because I learned to uncomplicate the process and to let nature do what nature does best. That is, I developed a system that provides the perfect environment for nature to do what nature has spent millions of years perfecting.

When I started to compost seriously, as an adult, I didn't actually have a garden. We were renting so I couldn't dig or plant in the yard or have a traditional compost pile.

So while I studied to get my Garden Landscape Certificate I thought that maybe I could at least try worm composting. I thought that would be a good start towards becoming a gardener.

> Moving compost, hauling compost, and turning compost is a lot of work. Not many people can do it and even fewer want to do it. Let the worms do it!

NO WORMS ALLOWED IN THE HOUSE

But my partner didn't want me to have worms in the house. So I tucked a couple of large plastic storage bins in the bushes and composted my food scraps in them. I made some basic mistakes but I learned from each one. The bins were so big, with so many food scraps in them, that the worms couldn't get to them all before they putrefied. I admit that was pretty gross. When I took the lid off to put in more food scraps the smell would almost knock me over. Also I had cut the bottoms completely out of the bins to give them contact with the soil. That made it difficult and really gross when the time came for us to move. Did I throw that mess away like a normal person? No I did not! I shoveled it into buckets and moved it to the new place like the composting ~~nut~~ hero that I am.

> Soon after I started food scrap composting, I found these giant writhing worm things in my bin. I thought that I had caused some mutant super bug to grow that was going to kill us all. Nope. Soldier Fly larvae are good guys.

PICKLED GARBAGE ALSO DIDN'T WORK FOR ME

I also experimented with a method called bokashi composting. Bokashi is a fermented wheat bran that pickles your food scraps so that supposedly they don't smell as bad while you are collecting them. I didn't like it. For one thing I think that they still smell strongly of pickled food scraps like onions, broccoli or whatever food you happen to have. And pickles. Plus it's an added expense, extra work and messy as it requires a drain for the black liquid that seeps out. And when I was trying to make it, I took a wrong turn that almost ended in my having to just tear my house down and build another one. That's a slight exaggeration, but it was bad.

You can buy bokashi. But I wanted to make it so that I could understand the whole process and because it's cheaper. To get a lower bulk price, I bought a 25 pound bag of wheat bran from the local feed store. It seems obvious now, in hindsight, that I didn't have to use the entire 25 pound bag on my first try, but I did.

SO, I FERMENTED THE WHOLE 25 POUND BAG OF WHEAT BRAN

in large plastic tubs. After a few days of fermenting I spread the bran out on a 10 foot tarp outside to dry. Then, because it looked like it might rain, I decided to bring everything inside and use a fan to dry it quicker. That turned out to be a big mistake.

The fan did dry the fermented wheat bran out. But it also blew a cheesy, yeasty, moldy bokashi smell onto everything in our house. I washed everything that was washable. I Lysoled and Febreezed everything that couldn't be wiped down. Every item of clothing in our closet smelled like it had been left wet in the washing machine for the hottest two weeks of the year. It took two washings just to make the clothes wearable. I swear they still smelled a little funky for weeks but maybe the smell was just stuck in my nose. I can laugh about it now but it was horrifyingly gross.

And it turns out that we don't need to pickle our garbage. We don't live that ancient lifestyle where this could actually be helpful. We have other needs to fit into our modern lifestyle and other tools we can use.

This is how nature composts.
It's messy, stinky and slow.
But it's also simple and easy.

> This is the fall remnants of last spring's garden experiment. I took my seeds and sprinkled them around on the soil. Stuff grew! The greens are still going strong. Overall I'm very happy with the return on time and effort invested.

WHY FOOD SCRAP COMPOSTING IS CRITICAL

This book is only about composting food scraps. Food waste, yard waste, and specialty wastes (like industrial or human waste) -each needs a different process to break it down successfully. Meaning that:

- it won't make a stinky mess
- it won't attract rats or racoons
- it's cheap
- it's easy
- it won't cause another problem.

The Constant Compost way is actually much easier than dealing with yard waste. You have lots of yard waste only a couple of times a year, but you have food scraps every day. You can't treat them like yard waste and expect good results. If you throw leftovers into your traditional yard pile they are going to stink and attract vermin. Things have to break down in order to compost. Decomposing leaves and sticks are earthy and pleasant, whereas rotting moldy food is not.

> Yard waste like leaves, weeds and sticks take a long time to break down. They are very tough and fibrous. Food scraps are mostly water and will break down quickly providing fast easy nutrition for your plants.

FOOD SCRAP COMPOSTING IS THE MOST NEGLECTED &

misunderstood aspect of composting. People try to gain some control of the process by using various methods such as indoor worm bins or technologies such as electric composters. Often you are trading one problem for another.

With worm bins you have to clean up after thousands of worms and their waste products. Food scraps can still smell, and the worms can escape or die on you. In the end you still have to sort the worms from their worm poo fertilizer.

In the case of electric composters, there is the smell of burning food scraps instead of rotting ones. Is that really better? Plus how environmentally friendly can it be when it's using electricity to literally cook all of the goodness and life out of your food scraps?

People won't continue composting when it is yucky and hard, and they may never try composting again after a bad experience. Composting in nature happens every day.

2

What is Constant Composting

> Those are worms coming in and out of my Origami Ruby Composter. The nice thing about free range worms is that you don't actually have to knit little hats for them or give them each individual names. Or touch them!

HOW TO USE THIS BOOK

It's your garden journey and this is your book. I hardly ever read a how-to book front to back, cover to cover, but it usually all gets read.

You can dog-ear the pages or write in it. In fact I have included some graph paper at the back for notes and drawings but margins and highlighting work too. A good hobby is all about the accessories so go nuts with the sticky place markers!

I have tried to keep it short and sweet with simple how-to line drawings where it counts. I want you to have a clear mental picture of the method before you start but I'm not trying to give you a full composting course.

I recommend that you try the method the way it is written before you start experimenting with it. The method works, but it's so different from most other ways of composting that you might be tempted to make changes before you even start. Don't. That will be defeating the whole point of what makes this method work and you will be disappointed.

> When you're composting food scraps in your garden bed you can, in fact you want, to plant right up next to it.
> The plants shelter the worms and the worms feed the plants.

YOU CAN'T FOOL NATURE

Constant Composting is so effective because it fully connects to nature instead of turning away from it as many modern processes do. We are not above or separate from nature, we are part of nature.

I met a gardener that had a phobia about dirt because it is, well, dirty. He paved his entire garden except small holes where the individual plants came through. I am not kidding. Not only was it quite bizarre looking but the life in the soil dies. Plants can't thrive cut off from the rain, sun and air. And they can't live in dead soil.

The soil is life for plants much like our own gut microbiome is for us. It supports the plants in complex ways we might never be able to fully understand or quantify.

I got to study hydroponic gardening in high school during the 1970s. At first I was very excited but in the end very unsatisfied. I didn't really know why at the time.

The 1970s hydroponic book that I was using looked

VERY HIPPIE
AND EARTHY

yet the whole thing was very removed from nature. The method had been reduced to just plants, water and the three main fertilizers known as NPK which stands for nitrogen, phosphorus and potassium. No soil. The clean roots of the plants were supported in sterile clay pellets.

Trying to grow plants on just chemical NPK is like trying to grow a child on only protein, sugar and fat that has been totally removed from real foods. Think burgers, sodas and fries. Yes, kids will grow and it's fine sometimes, but they need the vitamins, minerals, and fiber in real natural foods and good gut flora to become healthy adults.

And so do plants. We are learning that our gut contains a whole host of microorganisms that break down our food and then feed us. The soil is like that for plants. We are feeding the helpful microorganisms and invertebrates in the soil that then feed the plants.

And you know what else plants grown just on man made chemicals are missing? FLAVOR. That's right. The flavor of the fruit or vegetable comes from the care of the soil and every natural chemical that it provides for your plant.

HOW & WHY
CONSTANT COMPOSTING WORKS

I want you to be successful with your food scrap composting. Every aspect of my Constant Composting method has been well thought out and tested by myself and my family and friends.

The main idea is this: you provide the perfect insulated environment that's not too wet and not too dry, not too hot and not too cold. It slows down the temperature changes so the worms have time to move in and out of the bin and regulate their own comfort. And they can go out of the food scrap bin to deposit fertilizer (worm poo) in the collection bin or into your garden. Nobody, not even worms, likes poop on their food.

HELPFUL TERMS & CONCEPTS

My plan is to keep it simple and not give you a composting master course in this book, but in case you are completely unfamiliar with composting providing a few terms and concepts will be helpful:

- Bacteria - Microscopic one celled organisms.
- Compost - Decayed plant material used as fertilizer and soil improver.
- Decomposition - The breakdown of organic matter by invertebrates, bacteria and fungi.
- Earthworm - A common name for the soil-dwelling segmented worms that eat decaying plant and animal material. There are about 7000 species of earthworms.
- Earthworm Cocoons - Another name for earthworm eggs.
- Fungus - Yeasts, molds and mushrooms that help decompose and recycle organic matter and are vital to healthy plant growth. Plural is fungi.
- Invertebrates - An animal that doesn't have a backbone.
- Mulch is material spread on top of the soil.

- Organic - In chemistry organic means that a substance contains carbon atoms. In gardening organic means no synthetic chemicals are used.
- Organic Matter - refers to the products nature provides like leaves, sticks, animal waste that will compost.
- Red Wigglers - A type of earthworm that is very good at eating and processing food waste.
- Worm Castings - This is the technical name for worm poo. It is the stuff that builds healthy soil and provides the nutrients for your plants. It is the fertilizer that worms produce.
- Yard waste - Leaves, sticks, any leftover plant material after cleanup or gardening.

3
Let's Make a Food Scrap Composter

A protected gathering space for worms

SAFETY FIRST

When composting or working in dry soil don't breathe in the dust or funk. Composting is full of fungi and bacteria that are good for your soil, but probably not good for you to breathe, eat or get in any cuts you might have. Wear gloves, wash your hands after you finish. And ask your doctor about updating your tetanus shot. Be proactive about not overheating or getting sun stroke. Sometimes I move a big beach umbrella around and work under it. A cool rag on a hot day is a beautiful thing. Stay hydrated. Take frequent breaks to enjoy your handiwork.

A DETAILED OVERVIEW

There are only two main parts to the complete Constant Composting unit. A bottom collection bin and an insulated lid.

THE BOTTOM PART

The bottom collection bin has two parts; a food scrap collector that sits in a worm castings collector. It's made from two ordinary garden pots, one nested inside the other. This bottom collection bin is buried a few inches in the soil. The soil insulates it, allowing excess moisture to drain out and providing the worms with a place where they can go when the bin gets too hot or too cold.

THE TOP PART

The top is two nursery pots nested together and turned upside down to make a lid. It needs to be bigger around than the bottom pots so that it will fit down over them and rest on the soil.

The lid is made from two pots nested together with a layer of insulating bubble wrap in between. This slows down the temperature changes and gives the worms time to move in and out of the bottom composter bin, regulating their own comfort. The lid also keeps the odors inside so you don't smell it. And so that unwanted critters can't smell it either. In my experience if they can't smell it they don't bother it because they don't even know it's there.

THE GOLDILOCKS ZONE

This insulated safe zone is a food and rest area that allows the worms to be happy eating all of your food scraps. It's also ideal for earthworm reproduction to make more worms to eat even more food scraps.

Have you ever moved a flower pot, a moist brick or even a piece of wood that was sitting on concrete and found (or squished) worms living under it? They were under there because the conditions were perfect for them. It's damp and cool, but not too wet or too cold. They were protected from the heat. That is the Goldilocks zone environment you are providing for them but better because it's more spacious and has delicious food scraps. Plus no squishing happens.

THE TOP AND BOTTOM TOGETHER

Put your food scraps into that collection bin and cover it with the insulated lid. The worms will come in and eat your rotting food scraps. Then they will go in and out as they wish, stopping in the Goldilocks space between the two bottom pots, hanging out, making new baby worms and depositing some fertilizer in there.

That space between the pots is why you don't need bedding for your worms. Bedding (leaves, paper or cardboard) will slow down the process and in this system is completely unnecessary. You have provided your worms with the best, safest climate controlled rest area right next to their eating area.

At some point, once a month or once every few months, no rush, you can harvest the worm castings.

To harvest the fertilizer remove the inner pot full of food scraps and set it aside. Then remove the outer pot and dump the worm fertilizer around some plants. It's great for potted plants and houseplants. Then put the pots back in the soil and your worms are back in business. No sifting through icky stuff to get to the good stuff.

These are some worm castings that collected in an early experiment. It's got extra holes and pumpkin seeds!

DIAGRAMMED INSTRUCTIONS

FIRST A FEW PRO TIPS

Pro tip #1 -Have more than one unit. Your food scrap digester system will hold a couple of gallons of food scraps which will break down pretty quickly, depending on the season.

I like to have a couple of these going in every garden bed. They all have some food scraps in them so I have all of my garden beds being fertilized all the time by my worm army and I don't run out of room for my food waste.

Pro tip #2 - I'm giving you some nursery pot size measurements, but they don't have to be these exact sizes. The inner pots need to fit into the outer pots with a little empty space between them. And the lid pots have to fit, upside down over the bottom pots. That's it.

Because pots are made by different manufacturers they aren't perfectly sized. So you might end up with a 10 inch and 11 inch pots for the bottom and a 12 inch and 14 inch pots for the top. Or maybe 8 inch and 9.5 inch for the bottom and 10.5 and 12 inch for the top.

Sometimes two pots can have the same top measurements but because they are different styles they can have space between them at the sides and bottom. That will work too.

The top can be shorter than the bottom, as long as it fits over the bottom pots.

I dig around through my old pots and use whatever I have on hand. I love being able to reuse plastic. If you don't have any old pots try asking your friends and neighbors. There doesn't seem to be any shortage of used black nursery pots around.

Of course, decorative pots can work too. I would avoid anything too heavy. Remember, we are trying to keep this easy to use. And chances are your beautiful lush plants will grow up and hide most of it anyway.

Pro tip #3 - Do not add any more holes anywhere to any of the pots. Drain holes on the bottom or at the bottom edge are all that you need. For pots of this size, no other holes besides regular drain holes are necessary. Extra holes may cause the system to dry out too fast or to get too hot or too cold. Extra holes above the soil level can let out odors that may attract unwanted critters to your compost.

Don't worry, the system is not actually airtight. It won't become anaerobic as long as excess water can drain out of the bottom. And the worms will be able to breathe just fine without any extra holes. After all, they breathe when digging in the dirt.

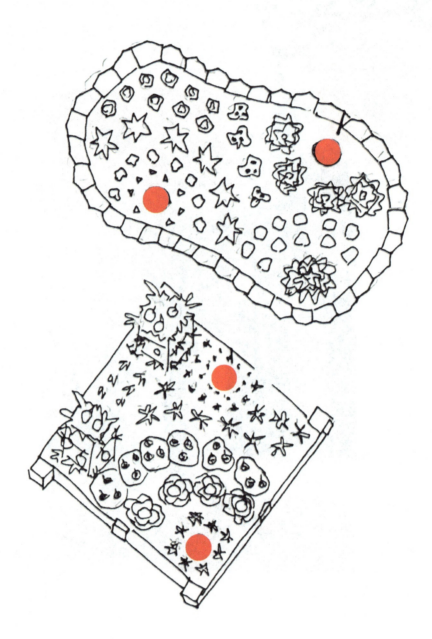

> These are some actual placements of Constant Composters in my garden. The red dots represent the composters. My plantings don't look this tidy. But my plants don't care, they give me food regardless.

Pro tip #4 - I used to locate my composter in the middle of my garden bed. That made visual sense to me. But I found that because the composter is low to the ground, this made it a little hard to reach, especially as my plants grew up around it. Over time this became just too annoying and I would procrastinate putting my food scraps in there. Now I locate the composter 6-12 inches from the side of the bed. This makes it much more convenient and easier to get the scraps in without making a mess.

Also you can plant right up next to it so it doesn't really take up much space. You can put shorter plants near the composter and plant the taller ones out towards the middle of the bed. If you have a square bed you can locate it in a corner or on the side. Leave 6-12 inches of soil around the outside edge for insulation. If you have a brick border around your garden bed that's good insulation too.

Plant around it in traditional rows, squares or in a rainbow shape. Or do my latest favorite thing and mix up your seeds, throw them out on the dirt and let nature sort it out. It's a time saver. I use an image search to identify the edible plants so I don't eat any toxic weeds.

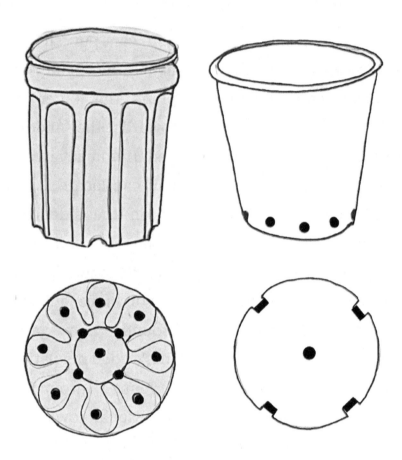

A Variety of Pots Will Work

You want excess water to drain out, so make sure the pots have several drain holes on the bottom. Also make sure that any side holes don't come too far up the side. You want any holes to be under the soil level. Side holes aren't necessary and don't make it work any better. I don't add side holes.

THE MATERIALS

1. One 9 inch and one 10 inch flower pot for the collection bin. The used ones that your plants come in from the nursery are fine. Must have several drain holes somewhere on or at the bottom. The holes must be low enough on the pot to sit a few inches below the soil line when the pot is buried. The newer flimsy flexible pots actually work well for collection bins.
2. Two larger flower pots for the lid, one bigger than the other. These must be large enough, when turned upside down, to fit over the bottom pots and rest on the ground. They can be shorter than the bottom pots but must be bigger around.
3. Bubble wrap, small or large, for the insulation in the lid. Plastic recycled mailing envelopes, like the ones you get from Amazon, work great.
4. Duct tape to join smaller pieces of bubble wrap together.
5. Scissors to trim the bubble wrap.
6. Two or three large binder clips to clip the two lid pots together. -NOTE: *Binder clips work if the pots are close to the same size and don't have a curved or cuffed lip on them. I*

63

have made a lid without any clips, just by securely jamming the pots together with the bubble wrap in between them. Also you can drill small holes into pots and zip tie them together with a dab of caulking to seal up the holes. This doesn't have to be perfect to work. You want the two lid pots to stay together and you don't want cold air to get in or smells to get out.

7. One cabinet pull knob of your choice. This is your chance to get fancy. They usually come with a flat screw. You will need a drill and bit to make a hole for this. I skip the drill when I can and get a short pointy screw that fits in my pull knob and use that to attach the knob to the lid. I use the point to screw it right through the pots. If the pots are very thick this doesn't work and I drill a hole. *NOTE: You can make it super easy and glue the knob to the lid.*

8. One flat washer, pretty much any size as long as it fits over the screw for the drawer pull knob without falling off on the inside.

9. Maybe a drill, drill bit, a little caulking or glue and a couple of zip ties depending on your pot and knob choices.

MAKING THE COLLECTOR BIN

1. Dig a hole 6-12 inches from the edge of your garden bed that's big enough for your largest bottom pot to sit down in the soil with the top 2 - 4 inches sticking up out of the ground.
2. Place the larger bottom pot in the soil and then place the smaller bottom pot inside of that one. Voila! Collection bin done.

    Your food scraps will go into this inner pot, and worm castings (fertilizer) will collect down in the larger pot.

3. To harvest worm castings, remove the inner pot full of food scraps and set it aside. Then pull out the bottom pot and dump the castings where you want extra fertilizing. They are great on potted plants. A sprinkle of worm castings will make your houseplants very happy. Replace the empty bottom pot back into the hole in the ground, then set the food scrap collection pot back inside the outer pot.

MAKING THE LID

1. Line the larger pot inside with one large piece of bubble wrap. Just set it on over the pot and jam it down in there like it was tissue paper in a gift bag. Make sure that it is large enough to stick out all along the pot edge.

I like to tape smaller used pieces of bubble wrap together to make one large square. Overlap any joining edges by an inch or so. You want the whole inside to be lined with bubble wrap with no gaps in between the pieces or at the edges where cold or hot air might get in.

2. Place the smaller pot firmly down inside the bubble wrap lined larger pot until the edges are even. Trim away the excess bubble wrap sticking out all around the edge. Secure the pots together with the binder clips. Flip the binder clip pincher wires forward to lie flat against the pot. You want the top edge of the pot lid to lie flat on the ground when you turn it over and place it over the food scrap collection bin.

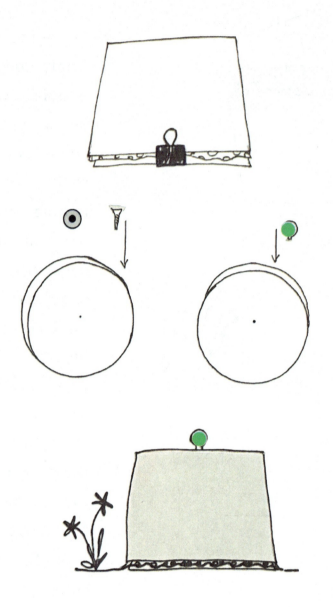

3. Now turn the pots upside down and this is the composter lid. Secure the knob to the top of the lid with the screw, using the washer inside to keep the screw from pulling through the pots. The plastic pots are pretty easy to screw into so I usually use a pointy screw to make my hole and attach the knob to it instead of the flat screw that came with the knob. I usually have an old screw laying around that will fit. But you can also use a drill to make a hole for the screw that came with the knob and use that. Or you can glue the knob on.

PUTTING IT ALL TOGETHER

So the bottom pots are in the ground with 2-4 inches sticking up out of the soil. The lid goes down over this with the edge fairly flat on the ground. It should lay flat enough against the ground that no obvious odors escape.

Now throw your food scraps in there and forget about them. Wondering what to feed your worms? Worms and other composting helpers will eat almost anything you will eat. Look for more details in the questions and answers section coming up.

If it seems dry inside the composter, add some water. Worms need some moisture. The excess will drain out and your plants will love it.

4

Start Composting

Feed your soil and it will feed your plants

COLLECTING FOOD SCRAPS

Having food scraps sit out in your kitchen can attract fruit flies and mold. It's definitely a composting turn-off. But there is an easy way to avoid this problem.

It's not often convenient for me to take food scraps right out to the bin. So I like to collect my food scraps in a recycled plastic bag and keep them in the freezer until I am ready to take them out to the composter. Freezing the food scraps means that I don't have to go out in the rain or the dark just to go to the composter. Or that I don't have to make a trip outside for one banana peel. Instead of several trips a day out to the composter I can go out once every couple of days.

Freezing food scraps has the added benefit of breaking down the food scraps a bit, making them rot faster so the worms can start chowing down sooner. I throw my frozen food scraps right in the composter. The worms will just avoid them until they are thawed out. That is the beauty of having a system where the worms can come and go as they please. Plus most of the year it's pretty hot where I am so frozen food scraps are more of a benefit than a problem.

WHAT TO PUT IN YOUR CONSTANT COMPOSTER

Any food will compost and you can put almost any kind of food into this system. However:

- BONES are going to take forever to break down. I would leave them out. You can bury them if you have room.
- EGGSHELLS also take a long time. They can be crushed up and sprinkled right on top of the soil.
- COFFEE GROUNDS. Worms love them but they don't need to take up room in your composter. They too can be sprinkled right on top of the soil.
- FAT, OIL or GREASE in large amounts is not a good idea, as worms breathe through their skin and can't breathe if they are smothered in oil.
- SALT doesn't compost and is not good for most plants or soil life. The normal amount in cooked food should not be a problem.
- PAPER TEA BAGS are fine, worms love them. I have put paper

takeout containers in my composter because I am lazy but the paper will take longer to break down.

- CHEESE and YOGURT in small amounts are fine.
- MILK can be watered down and poured directly on shrubs or trees, not in the composter.
- FRUIT JUICES are too acidic for plants or the food scrap composter. Fruit is fine. Worms love fruit. Banana peels are a good way to attract worms to your composter.
- VINEGAR has way too much acid and will burn your worms. And vinegar isn't good for your plants either. A little ketchup on fries or a pickle slice is fine.
- SUGAR OR CANDY. Worms, fungus and bacteria love this stuff as much as we do.
- ONIONS. Normal amounts of onion are fine. A lot of onions, citrus or a lot of any one food such as you have with canning may slow the system down while the worms adjust but they will get used to it. New worms that hatch with an abundance of that food will be particularly fond of it.
- MOLDY FOOD is fine to put in. Mold is the first part of the composting process.

- PAPER, like the occasional napkin or a tissue is fine, but it will be slower to compost. If it was alive it will compost. Paper was alive as it comes from trees and trees were definitely alive. But wood, and therefore paper, is full of fibers that are hard to break down.

If you want to compost more paper you can do that with leaves or yard waste. Paper or bedding of any kind, like leaves for instance, is not necessary in this setup and will slow the process.

QUESTIONS AND ANSWERS

Q. Can I add composting worms to my composter?

A. Yes you can. Your native soil worms might not work as fast as composting worms but they will work. Food scraps are full of water so they break down pretty quickly just by rotting. Other things like fungus, bacteria and other soil bugs help with the process too.

You can buy composting worms at bait shops or garden centers.

Q. I added my food scraps and nothing seems to be happening. What's up?

A. The system takes a while to get started. It's a process. The food scraps have to actually break down (rot) a bit for the worms to eat them. Worms need to discover the food and move in. Give it time.

Fruit peels are especially attractive to worms so if you want to lure them in make sure to add some banana or other fruit.

It might take the adult worms a while to learn to love your food, just like sometimes it takes people a while to learn to love a new food.

Also, just like we tend to love the foods of our childhood, the new worms that hatch out in your food waste are going to really love it no matter what it is.

Remember that this system is designed to be used in a raised garden bed that gets watered on a fairly regular basis. If it gets too dry that will slow down or halt the process. Your worms will not be happy and they will leave.

If the soil doesn't drain, your worms will leave. Worms need to be moist but they need oxygen too as they breathe through their skin.

Q. How long will it take to make compost?

A. It will take as long as it takes. Try not to worry about that. The worms are doing all the work so relax and let it do its thing. Your Constant Composting system is actually making compost all the time.

The point of this method is not actually the harvesting of worm fertilizer, but the fact that the worms do all the work so you can do other things. The harvestable worm castings are an added bonus.

You can harvest worm castings out of the bottom pot whenever you want. I harvest mine about every six months because I am busy. But you can check on it anytime you want and use what is there.

Worm castings are great for houseplants, your potted plants outside, your vegetable or flower garden. You can mix some into potting soil for starting seeds or repotting.

Also worm castings act as an insect repellent in the soil. They really are black garden gold.

NATURES COMPOSTERS

You might see these hard working bugs
But you don't have to touch them
Unless you want to

	Pill Bugs are also called Woodlice and are related to crabs and lobsters	Fruit Flies love fruit like you do
Earthworms or Composting Worms are the celebrities of composting	Soldier flies and thier larvae look scary but they are harmless	Grubs can be good or bad but they are great composters and birds love them
Pincher Bugs eat dead plants and animals They are your clean-up crew		Various beetles like Ground Beetles and Cockroaches love to eat your leftovers
	Slugs, not great anywhere but in the compost bin	

Q. I went out to my composter and it was full of a certain bug (fruit flies, sow bugs, giant wriggly larvae things, pincher bugs, beetles.) What should I do?

A. Probably nothing. These are all composting helpers. They will come and go as the food in your bin changes. Aren't you glad that you don't have to touch them?

The first time that I went out to my food scrap compost and saw that it was full of the giant wriggling larvae of soldier flies, I thought that I had caused something to breed that was going to kill us all! But in fact soldier fly larvae are excellent composters and adult soldier flies, while they look mean, can't even bite. At all. Now I love it when they show up.

The only bugs that I do anything to control are ants and roaches. While these are also natural and will help to compost, I find that ants eventually kill the plants they are nesting in. And I don't want ants or roaches in my house, which is a problem where I live. I use sticky roach traps, diatomaceous earth and borax ant bait traps to control these pests.

Q. I filled up my composter. What happens if my family generates too many food scraps for my composter?

Do a Happy Dance and make another one. This is an opportunity to fertilize another spot. Plan on one composter per person depending on lifestyle and eating/cooking habits, or more. It doesn't hurt to have more of them and for them to be only half full. More composters means more areas are getting fertilized.

5
Happy Composting

It doesn't have to be perfect to work

HAPPY CONSTANT COMPOSTING

I hope that you had fun reading this little book and thinking about how the Constant Composting method will fit into your lifestyle and benefit your garden.

But more than that, I hope that you will actually give food scrap composting a try. You will have taken a small but important step in leaving a smaller footprint on the planet.

The average person is estimated to generate upwards of 250 pounds of food waste a year. That's 1000 pounds for a family of four. And you are now using yours to nourish the earth. Don't you feel better? I do.

I wish you lots of success on your journey to making rich soil and growing healthy, beautiful and delicious plants.

The following journal pages are a little bonus for you. You can keep track of your composting efforts, draw out a garden plan, dream, wish, set goals, paste pictures and seed packets. Do whatever you want with those pages. Enjoy!

This Food Scrap Compost
Journal Belongs to

_____

Started on _____/_____/_____

In _____